Reading for Every Child
Fluency

Grade 4

by
Susan J. Herron

Published by Instructional Fair
an imprint of
Frank Schaffer Publications®

Instructional Fair

Author: Susan J. Herron
Editor: Rebecca Warren
Interior Designer: Lori Kibbey

Frank Schaffer Publications®

Instructional Fair is an imprint of Frank Schaffer Publications.

Printed in the United States of America. All rights reserved. Limited Reproduction Permission: Permission to duplicate these materials is limited to the person for whom they are purchased. Reproduction for an entire school or school district is unlawful and strictly prohibited. Frank Schaffer Publications is an imprint of School Specialty Children's Publishing. Copyright © 2005 School Specialty Children's Publishing.

Send all inquiries to:
Frank Schaffer Publications
3195 Wilson Drive NW
Grand Rapids, Michigan 49544

Reading for Every Child: Fluency—grade 4

ISBN: 0-7424-2824-9

1 2 3 4 5 6 7 8 9 10 PAT 10 09 08 07 06 05 04

Table of Contents

Reading First 4
Getting the Facts on Fluency 5-7
Assessing Fluency 8-9
NAEP Oral Reading Fluency Scale 10
Reading Fluency Rubric 11
Fluency Self-Assessment 12-13
Instructional Strategies for Fluency 14
Tape-Assisted Reading 15-16
Silent Reading 17
Modeled Fluent Reading 18
Choral Reading 19
    Family 20
    Show-Offs 21
Echo Reading 22
    Homework 23
    Time for School 24
Repeated Reading 25-26
    Performing Poetry 27
    Cleaning 28-30
    Catch Up!? 31-33
    The Perfect Meal 34-36
Expressive Reading 37-39
    It's a Bird! It's a Plane! It's a . . . Penguin? 40-42
Readers' Theater 43-46
    The Great Cake Taker 47-55
    Student Evaluation Form for Readers' Theater 56
Partner Reading 57-58
    Invisible 59-61
Fluency Development Lesson 62
    Bubble, Bubble, Toil and Trouble 63-65
    Washington and Lincoln 66-68
Comprehension 69-70
    Tips 71
    Directions 72
    Dilemma 73-76
Resources 77-79
Answer Key 80

Reading First

Introduction
The "Reading First" program is part of the No Child Left Behind Act. This program is based on research by the National Reading Panel that identifies five key areas for early reading instruction—phonemic awareness, phonics, fluency, vocabulary, and comprehension.

Phonemic Awareness
Phonemic awareness focuses on a child's understanding of letter sounds and the ability to manipulate those sounds. Listening is a crucial component, as the emphasis at this level is on sounds that are heard and differentiated in each word the child hears.

Phonics
After students recognize sounds that make up words, they must then connect those sounds to *written* text. An important part of phonics instruction is systematic encounters with letters and letter combinations.

Fluency
Fluent readers are able to recognize words quickly. They are able to read aloud with expression and do not stumble over words. The goal of fluency is to read more smoothly and with *comprehension*.

Vocabulary
In order to understand what they read, students must first have a solid base of vocabulary words. As students increase their vocabulary knowledge, they also increase their comprehension and fluency.

Comprehension
Comprehension is "putting it all together" to understand what has been read. With both fiction and nonfiction texts, students become active readers as they learn to use specific comprehension strategies before, during, and after reading.

Getting the Facts on Fluency

Defining Fluency

Fluency is defined as "the ability to read a text accurately and quickly," according to *Put Reading First*, a document published by the Partnership for Reading and funded by the National Institute for Literacy (NIFL). Timothy V. Rasinski, in his book *From Phonics to Fluency*, defines fluency as the ability to "to read expressively, meaningfully, in appropriate syntactic units (phrases, clauses), at appropriate rates, and without word recognition difficulty."

Fluency involves accuracy, expression, phrasing, speed, and automaticity (fast, effortless word recognition). Fluent readers sound as if they were engaged in conversation.

Fluency provides a bridge between word recognition and comprehension. Fluent readers are not focused on decoding. Their attention is on making connections between the text and their own prior knowledge. They are making meaning from print—comprehending it. As you are reading right now, you are decoding words automatically while comprehending the text. You are performing two or more complex tasks simultaneously. Less fluent readers are focused on decoding (word recognition) to such a degree that little attention can be given to making meaning. Comprehension suffers. You can hear laborious word-by-word reading as they move through the text with little expression or understanding. Even one task is difficult for these readers.

Acquiring Fluency

Many factors contribute to the acquisition of fluency. Some children come from homes where stories, nursery rhymes, and poems are read to them from the moment they arrive home from the hospital—and even before that! Lap reading is extremely important in developing concepts of print and in hearing fluent reading modeled. Children who come from homes that are "print rich" are exposed to multiple experiences with good reading habits and many opportunities to recite familiar text. Have you listened to young children who memorize a favorite book and "read" it aloud? They have had many occasions to reread the same passages. Reading with expression is learned by mimicking the way a parent or other experienced reader reads a story.

Finding Text at the Right Text Level

Successful readers read text at a level that is easy for them and develops confidence in both fluency and comprehension. Fluent readers do more independent reading and read more for pleasure; the more they read, the better they become at recognizing words and making meaning from print.

Fluent readers read faster, more accurately, in phrases, and with intonation. Reading rate is one general measure of fluency. As children progress, the number of words read per minute (wpm) increases. Even though slower readers may spend more time on the task, they probably comprehend less. Richard L. Allington (2001) found that struggling readers are more likely to be reading materials that are too difficult, more likely to be asked to read aloud, more likely to be interrupted when they misread a word, and more likely to wait for the teacher's prompt. Struggling readers are frequently given a word they do not know. The problem is they learn to anticipate that this will be done for them. This behavior fosters more word-by-word reading as they await reassurance from another reader.

Fluency can change in certain situations. A very effective fluent reader can become less fluent if presented with a highly technical text containing unfamiliar words and ideas. In that situation, reading becomes slow, labored, and very focused on word recognition as the reader struggles along. Reading with meaning is certainly compromised. Knowing that any fluent reader can become less fluent when reading difficult or unfamiliar text makes us aware of the necessity of providing text at appropriate levels—even below grade level—for the purpose of teaching fluency.

Struggling readers read less than more successful readers because they often cannot read classroom basal text or anthologies or engage in reading other text independently. This situation widens the gap between the readers. Readers need to practice reading at a level where they feel safe and comfortable with text. Increased independent reading results in increased word recognition. Increased word recognition leads to more fluent reading and improved comprehension.

Conversely, if a child's energy is spent identifying words, his or her comprehension and response to the text is hindered. According to Nathan and Stanovich (1991), "When processes of word recognition take little capacity (are fluent), most of the reader's cognitive capacity can be focused on comprehending the text, criticizing it, elaborating on it, and reflecting on it—in short, doing all the things we know good readers do" (p. 176). And, according to the National Reading Panel (2000), "Children who do not develop reading fluency, no matter how bright they are, will continue to read slowly and with great effort."

Using Technology to Develop Fluency

Because of advances in technology, there are now many electronic books on the market. For struggling readers, the listening version provides the read-aloud piece while the student follows along with the written text. When students access individual words on demand, the supported text acts as if a fluent reader were assisting the reader. Materials at the listening level can be read easily. Fluency, sight word vocabulary, and comprehension can be improved by using computerized text.

CD-ROM interactive talking books are digital versions of stories that incorporate animation, music, sound effects, and highlighted text. They support the development of literacy by allowing students to listen to the story, read along with the story, echo read, and participate as different characters in a digital readers' theater.

Setting Fluency Standards

Fluency is a benchmark in most academic content standards for English language arts. Through the school year, fourth-grade fluent readers should increase their rate of oral reading, increase sight vocabulary, read more demanding text with greater ease, show appropriate pause, pitch, stress, and intonation, and increase proficiency in silent reading. The activities in this book will help your students meet that standard.

Assessing Fluency

Assessment drives instruction. This section gives the teacher and the student tools for assessing fluency. Students should be formally assessed for fluency on a regular basis. Teachers can listen to students read orally during independent reading time, at a conference, or from a taped recording. More formal measures, such as measuring oral reading rate and checking comprehension should be included as well.

Words per Minute

Oral reading rate is the number of words correctly read in one minute. You can assess a child's oral reading rate in the following manner. The procedure is simple and is done during a one-minute reading. The steps are:

- Select a brief passage from a grade-level text.
- Count the words in the passage.
- Ask the student to read the passage aloud. Time the student for **exactly** one minute while you track the number of errors in the reading.
- Count the total number of words the student read.
- Count the number of errors the student made.
- Subtract the number of errors from the total number of words read in one minute.
- The result is the WCPM (words correct per minute).

The formula looks like this:

Total number of words read: _____ – **errors:** _____ = words read correctly, the WCPM

Repeat this procedure at intervals throughout the year and record results on a graph. Results can be compared with published norms or standards.

Fourth-grade oral fluency norms look like this:

Grade 4 percentile	WCPM		
	fall	winter	spring
75%	125	133	143
50%	99	112	118
25%	72	89	92

Source: "Curriculum-Based Oral Reading Fluency Norms for Students in Grades 2 Through 5," by J. E. Hasbrouck and G. Tindal in *Teaching Exceptional Children*, Vol. 24, Spring 1992, 41–44.

Multidimensional Fluency Scale

Zutell and Rasinski (1991) developed the Multidimensional Fluency Scale (MFS) as a practical measurement of a student's oral fluency. The scale rates a reader on pace (rate), smoothness (automatic word recognition), and phrasing. See the bibliography on page 77 for information on how to find this scale. (The scale is found in *Goodbye Round Robin* by Opitz and Rasinski.)

Assessment Kits and Rubrics

Commercially prepared assessment materials are available. Kits include materials such as manuals, passages for reading, progress charts, rubrics, and even timers. Rubrics for rating fluency are available online and in books you can purchase. Page 11 of this book contains a sample fluency rubric. See the resources section beginning on page 77 for additional sources.

Audio Recordings

You can have your students record their reading of a passage on tape so that you can assess it together for fluency, accuracy, pacing, intonation, and expression.

The important thing about assessment is to do it on a regular basis and to give your students feedback on their progress while you are tracking their development and making informed decisions about instruction.

NAEP Oral Reading Fluency Scale

Level 4	Reads primarily in larger, meaningful phrase groups. Although some regressions, repetitions, and deviations from text may be present, these do not appear to detract from the overall structure of the story. Preservation of the author's syntax is consistent. Some or most of the story is read with expressive interpretation.
Level 3	Reads primarily in three- or four-word phrase groups. Some smaller groupings may be present. However, the majority of phrasing seems appropriate and preserves the syntax of the author. Little or no expressive interpretation is present.
Level 2	Reads primarily in two-word phrases with some three- or four-word groupings. Some word-by-word reading may be present. Word groupings may seem awkward and unrelated to larger context of sentence or passage.
Level 1	Reads primarily word by word. Occasional two-word or three-word phrases may occur, but these are infrequent and/or they do not preserve meaningful syntax.

Source: U.S. Department of Education, National Center for Education Statistics. *Listening to Children Read Aloud,* 15. Washington, D.C.: 1995.

Reading Fluency Rubric

Areas Scored	3—Outstanding	2—Right on Track	1—Push a Little Harder!
Fluency	Smooth, connected reading with appropriate pauses; no hesitations or stops. Meaning is maintained.	Some inappropriate pauses; occasional hesitation or stops. Meaning is sometimes blurred; occasional choppiness.	Hesitation in every line, many false starts and awkward pauses. Meaning is not maintained, with frequent guessing of words.
Phrasing	Consistently chunks text and follows punctuation. Groups words logically.	Some inappropriate phrasing; follows punctuation. Usually groups words logically.	Reads word by word; ignores phrasing and punctuation. No logical grouping.
Rate	Reads at appropriate speed.	Sometimes maintains appropriate speed.	Does not select appropriate speed.
Expression	Adjusts tone, inflection, stress, and expression to match meaning of the passage.	Sometimes adjusts tone, inflection, stress, and expression to match meaning of the passage.	Does not recognize use of tone, inflection, stress, and expression to match meaning of the passage. Reads in a monotone.
Oral Interpretation	Incorporates oral interpretation of text.	Oral interpretation is not always evident.	Oral interpretation is not evident.
Self-Monitoring	Employs self-monitoring skills to check for accuracy.	Sometimes employs self-monitoring skills to check for accuracy.	Does not employ self-monitoring skills.
Comprehension	Demonstrates understanding of the selection.	Demonstrates some understanding of the selection.	Poor understanding of the selection.

Published by Instructional Fair. Copyright protected. 0-7424-2824-9 Reading for Every Child: Fluency

Fluency Self-Assessment

Helping Your Students Self-Assess

Students need to see their growth over time and to be aware of their strengths and weaknesses. There are several ways to accomplish this.

- Students can **graph** their reading rates (speed) and accuracy. Each student keeps a graph tracking of the number of words per minute he or she is reading on a given day or the number of correct words read. A bar graph works well. Reading partners can time each other with a stopwatch and also record errors by using a copy of the text being read. The graph provides concrete evidence of accomplishment. When setting a time goal, encourage speed over accuracy and a goal of 85 words per minute. Successive readings (three) of the same selection can be recorded.

- Students can **answer comprehension questions** about passages they read. This can be done with a partner, in a teacher conference, or as a written exercise. See the student activities on pages 71–76 for sample passages and questions.

- Students can **read a selection and record it on tape**. They can gain insight into their own reading by hearing it. Comments on the reading can be shared with the teacher or reading partner. When students reread the selection after practice, they can monitor their own progress.

- Students can **complete a checklist** or evaluation of their reading, especially after hearing a taped recording (see page 13).

- Students can assess themselves or a partner with a **rubric** (see pages 10–11).

Name _____ Date _____

Name of Passage _____

Fluency Self-Assessment Checklist

Answer the following questions after you read a passage and/or section of a book.

1. I read smoothly, as if I were speaking.

    yes   sometimes   no

2. I read the way the character would sound and expressed the character's feelings with my voice.

    yes   sometimes   no

3. I paid attention to punctuation and phrasing, altering my pace.

    yes   sometimes   no

4. I understood what I read.

    yes   sometimes   no

5. I corrected mistakes quickly.

    yes   sometimes   no

Instructional Strategies for Fluency

Fluency instruction cannot be neglected in a comprehensive reading program. Direct reading instruction results in the greatest fluency growth for struggling readers. Students need to have expressive, fluent, and meaningful reading **modeled** for them. Notice that **reading aloud** is an important part of most reading programs. Students derive great joy in listening to the teacher read to the class. Many teachers read as a way to relax and regroup after lunch or at the end of a day. Text read to the class can be at a much higher level than text used for instruction or independent reading. It's a fantastic way to enhance vocabulary for all learners—but most especially for auditory learners.

Fluency involves more than just accurate word recognition. It also incorporates reading **speed**. Timothy Rasinski's article "Speed Does Matter in Reading" in *The Reading Teacher* (2000), addresses the question of reading rate. He reminds us that slow readers invest more time and energy in a reading task than more fluent readers. Sometimes the slower reader simply pretends to be finished with the assignment in order to avoid standing out as the last one to finish. For slow readers, simple assignments become laborious and can result in poor comprehension and poor reading performance.

Students must have many opportunities to **practice** reading and to have **support** while they are reading. The good news is that reading fluency and improved rate can be developed through instructional strategies that support the goal of creating fluent readers who read quickly, accurately, expressively, and with little effort, performing multiple tasks simultaneously.

Instructional strategies for fluency include:

- tape-assisted reading
- silent reading
- modeled fluent reading
- choral reading
- echo reading
- rereading/repeated reading
- expressive reading
- readers' theater
- paired reading
- fluency development lessons
- comprehension

Tape-Assisted Reading

One version of assisted, supported reading is listening to books on tape and following along in the text. Readers who may not be able to read a text independently can benefit from hearing a fluent reader read. Books should be at the student's **independent reading level** and read at a rate of about 80–100 words per minute.

The first reading should involve the reader listening only while following along in the text. During subsequent readings, the student should **read along with the tape**. Tapes provide reinforcement for auditory learners and create an opportunity to increase vocabulary by compensating for differences between reading and listening vocabularies. The goal is to have students read the text independently without support after a number of rereadings.

Sources for Audio Recordings

Commercially prepared books and tapes are readily available; however, often the reader reads too quickly and, even when signals to turn the page are present, students find it difficult to keep up. Ideally the classroom teacher, tutors, parents, or older (more fluent) students would prepare the recording. The downside of using tapes is that sometimes students only listen to the text and never look at the print. This really defeats the purpose, which is to allow readers to see and hear words simultaneously.

Equipment for Listening Center

You will need an audiocassette recorder with a microphone and blank tapes. The best tape players for classroom use are individual cassette players without radios. You will need a good supply of batteries or rechargeable batteries and a charger. The headsets can be stored on small plastic hooks to keep them from getting all tangled up. I acquired clear plastic backpacks for storing cassette players, books, and tapes by requesting them in a grant proposal I wrote. Don't overlook grant writing as a wonderful way to fill your wish list!

Audio taping can be used to collect samples of a student's fluency growth over time. The student can select a favorite text to read silently, then aloud (at least three times) before making a tape. He or she can record the oral reading, noting the date of the recording and any other information you want to include.

Allington (1999) describes a technique called "Tape, Check, Chart" in his book *What Really Matters for Struggling Readers*. Students tape their reading of a passage. They then replay the tape while following along with a photocopy of the text. All mispronounced words are given a small check in black ink. After a second reading, they listen again. This time mispronounced words are given a red check. After a third reading, misreads are marked in blue or green. Successive readings should indicate fewer mistakes each time the passage is read. Students can readily see their progress.

Best Books on Tape for Fourth-Grade Students

Bunting, Eve. *The Summer of Riley*. Read by Ramon de Ocampo. Recorded Books.

Cooper, Susan. *Silver on the Tree*. Read by Alex Jennings. Listening Library.

Creech, Sharon. *Ruby Holler*. Read by Donna Murphy. Harper Audio.

Dahl, Roald. *Boy*. Read by Derek Jacobi. Harper Audio.

Fleischman, Paul. *Seek*. Read by a full cast. Listening Library.

Frady, Marshall. *Martin Luther King, Jr.* Read by Marshall Frady. Books on Tape.

Halberstam, David. *Firehouse*. Read by Mel Foster. Brilliance Audio.

Hunt, Irene. *Across Five Aprils*. Read by Terry Bregy. Audio Bookshelf.

Lewis. C. S. *The Lion, the Witch, and the Wardrobe*. Read by a full cast. Focus on the Family/Tyndale House, Family Listening.

Osborne, Mary Pope. *American Tall Tales*. Read by Scott Snively. Audio Bookshelf.

Park, Linda Sue. *A Single Shard*. Read by Graeme Malcolm. Listening Library.

Singer, Nicky. *Feather Boy*. Read by Philip Franks. Listening Library.

Spinelli, Jerry. *Maniac Magee*. Read by S. Epatha Merkerson. Listening Library.

Silent Reading

The National Reading Panel, a congressionally mandated independent panel formed to review the scientific literature and determine the most effective ways to teach children to read, concluded that guided oral reading is important in developing reading fluency. In guided reading, students read aloud and are provided with feedback.

In contrast, the panel was not able to determine if silent reading helped improve fluency. Good readers read silently more than less fluent readers and they also read more often. Does independent reading improve reading skills, or do good readers just prefer reading to themselves? There has not been enough conclusive research to make a definite conclusion. That does not mean, however, that silent reading has no value. Spending time with texts that each student has chosen for pleasure helps develop a positive attitude toward reading. Silent reading should be included as part of a balanced reading program.

How to Include Silent Reading Time in Your Day

Silent reading should have a place in the daily schedule. Some teachers like to begin the day with silent reading, some prefer time after lunch, and others schedule time at the end of the day. Some teachers call it DEAR time (Drop Everything and Read) while others call the time SSR (Sustained Silent Reading).

During this time (15–20 minutes), the teacher and students read a book, a newspaper, or a magazine of their own choosing. The teacher reads at the same time. This is not a time for grading papers or for students to complete homework. There are no interruptions; it is a quiet time. The emphasis is on the joy of reading for pleasure, and students are not asked to report on what they read. In some classrooms, book discussions occur once a week so students can talk about what they are reading. After all, many of us read books others have recommended! Time spent reading during the silent reading period can actually increase time spent reading at home as well.

Modeled Fluent Reading

As the classroom teacher, you are the model for reading. It is your expressive oral reading that tells your students what fluent reading sounds like. They learn how a reader's voice helps make meaning from the text. They hear how characters come to life and how emotions are shared with the listener. Parents, family members, tutors, older students, and peers can also model good reading.

Reading aloud to students is an important piece of literacy instruction. It enables them to hear fluent reading and transfer what they learn to their own reading. Read-aloud time and the accompanying discussion and support help students to appreciate text that may be above their independent reading level. They can be exposed to a wide variety of genres including speeches, poetry, fables, and folk tales.

If readers are grouped by ability or reading level, hearing fluent reading modeled is essential. A teacher can participate in reading aloud with students in the group. After modeling, engage students in discussion about what good readers do.

Classroom Activities for Modeled Reading

Using modeled reading can be as simple as reading aloud to students. You can extend this exercise with some simple activities.

- Have students follow along with a copy of the text you are reading aloud. Connecting what they hear to the printed text links words to sounds in their minds and helps increase comprehension.

- As you read, ask students to circle any words they do not know. When you are finished reading, students look up the words. Then you read the passage a second time.

- To get students thinking about expression, have them underline any places where you said something loudly, put a slash mark where you paused, and a star where you changed your voice to show another character. Compare notes as a class and discuss the role of punctuation in making meaning.

# Choral Reading

Choral reading involves an entire group or class reading the same text aloud at the same time (in unison). All students are active participants and must be able to see a copy of the printed text. Less fluent readers are more willing to participate because they are not reading in isolation and their peers support them in their oral reading. However, if students are reluctant to read, they can join in by first reading just words they know. Choral readings can be done with anthologies, poems, song lyrics, or trade books. Select text that is not too long and is at the independent or instructional level for most students. Reading with more fluent readers increases comprehension for those who struggle.

Generally, the teacher is the lead voice. Variations of choral reading can be done using high and low voices, soft and loud voices, solo or multiple voices, or few voices building to many voices.

For example:

- The teacher reads the body of a poem and the class reads the refrain in unison.
- The class separates into two groups and each one reads a line of the poem.
- One student begins and other students join in as each line is read.

Tape recordings can also be used for practice. Tape the whole class reading the text several different times so they can compare their progress. After reading a selection from three to five times—not all at one time—students should be able to read it independently. For some sample texts to use with choral reading, see the activities on pages 20–21.

Family

Directions: First, listen to your teacher read this poem. Pay careful attention to the expression and speed of the reading. Which words are emphasized? Then read the poem in unison, with all of you reading together. Practice reading the poem several times until you are able to read it on your own.

1	It might be two,
2	It might be four, or maybe more,
3	Family.
4	Support and love—
5	That's what I think of,
6	And sometimes a fight or two.
7	Taking a walk with you,
8	Helping you if you're feeling blue,
9	Family.
10	All different,
11	Yet the same,
12	Loving one another,
13	Family.
14	Brother, sister,
15	Mother, father,
16	Grandmother, grandfather,
17	Aunt, uncle,
18	Special friend,
19	Family.

Show-Offs

Directions: Read the following passage as a group. After you have read it aloud the first time, talk about which lines should be slow or fast, which should be loud or soft, and which words you do not know. Practice reading aloud several different times as a group until you can tell the story with style!

I have always hated show-offs. Just because you can do something well doesn't mean you should make other people feel inferior. Devan is the biggest show-off I know. He thinks he's the skating KING or something. Well, he *used* to think that. You won't believe what happened to him!

It was the day Devan set up a race for all of us skaters who hang around at the park. There was only one rule—first one to the hot dog stand wins. We set off in a pack, but before we had gotten very far, Devan veered off the path and skated onto the grass as smoothly as if he were gliding on ice. None of us could skate on the grass without falling right down. As he rushed past us, Devan turned back and laughed with a mocking sneer.

"Forget him," I said to my friend Tashara. "Keep going!" We weren't the fastest, but we weren't the slowest, either. You should have seen us go! One after another, we pushed and pushed till everything was a blur around us and the wind was fast in our faces. We sped along, moving closer and closer to the front of the pack.

We turned the corner by the swings and all of a sudden—we did it! We were finally the leaders! Only a few more feet to go when— WHAM! Out of the grass beside us came Devan, shouting loudly, "I'm going to win—I got here first!!" just in time to smash into the hot-dog cart and land with his face in a tub of pickles.

"Well," Tashara said to me after we helped Devan up, "I guess we won't have to worry about show-offs any more!"

Echo Reading

Echo reading is another form of supported reading. The teacher reads several sentences, a paragraph, or a page aloud and the student(s) immediately read back what the teacher has read. Echo reading focuses on the teacher's modeling of fluent reading. Unlike choral reading, where the class reads the text in unison, echo reading allows for **instant repetition** of the same lines after the teacher has read it through once. The phrasing and pronunciation are fresh in student minds as they repeat each section piece by piece. You can group the text by stanzas, sentences, or the person who is speaking.

Combining Echo Reading and Choral Reading

It may be helpful to combine both echo reading and choral reading with the same text. You can first read the text together as a whole (choral reading) and then focus in on specific sections (echo reading). Include trade and nonfiction books for echo reading; these should be at an instructional level, where new words are introduced. Using echo reading can move your struggling readers to greater fluency as they get repeated exposure to texts that may be above their independent reading level.

Echo Reading as Preparation for Readers' Theaters

Because echo reading focuses so closely on smaller units of text, students can pay special attention not only to the words but also to the **expression** with which those words are communicated. When preparing for readers' theaters, try using echo reading with the different characters as a way to help your students practice their parts.

Homework

Directions: First, your teacher will read a stanza of the poem to you. Then you will repeat that same stanza back to your teacher. Listen carefully to your teacher's speed and expression while he or she is reading this poem. Notice how punctuation can help you understand a poem by telling you when to stop (at a period) and when to keep going (at a comma). Sometimes a sentence in a poem continues over several lines. In those cases, you should not stop after each line.

1	Heavy in my backpack,
2	Making me so blue,
3	Instead of running out to play,
4	It's what I have to do—
5	Homework, homework, homework.
6	Dad says I must do it.
7	He will not give me a break.
8	I guess I'll be stuck in my room
9	With that burden I can't shake—
10	Homework, homework, homework.
11	I dive into the workbook
12	And do each task I see.
13	It's not too long and then I'm done.
14	The rest of today I'm totally free.
15	No more homework for me!

Time for School

Directions: Listen to your teacher read each short passage about a student getting ready for school in the morning. Notice the speed and expression your teacher uses while reading. After your teacher has finished each passage, you take a turn reading. Which student is most like you? Why?

Troy

"Dad, where is my green shirt?"

"Try the laundry room," Troy's dad shouts back, trying to sound patient.

"I already looked and I can't find it in there!"

"Maybe it's dirty," Troy's father offers.

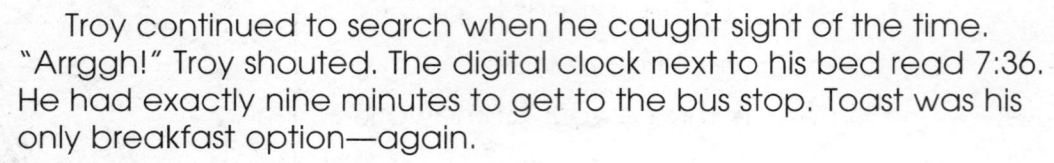

Troy continued to search when he caught sight of the time. "Arrggh!" Troy shouted. The digital clock next to his bed read 7:36. He had exactly nine minutes to get to the bus stop. Toast was his only breakfast option—again.

José

The alarm sounded early. José wanted to pull the covers over his head and go back to sleep, but he knew his coach was counting on him. He jumped up and pulled on his sweats and running shirt. Yikes! It was cold inside. José shuddered to think about how cold it might be outside. The poster on his wall said one word, "Dedication." Jose knew he had it. He would arrive to run with his teammates at 5:30 A.M., two hours before the first bus full of his classmates arrived. He grabbed a banana on his way out the door.

Isabelle

"Stop torturing me!" Isabelle shouted. Her brother loved to wake her up by throwing stuffed animals at her bed. Once Tom ran out of her room, Isabelle dragged herself out of bed and yawned. She would finish up the last page of her math homework while she ate breakfast. Mom had made her favorite breakfast—scrambled eggs and a bagel. Should she walk to school today or ride her bike? She had plenty of time to decide. She wouldn't leave for school for another thirty minutes.

 **Fluency**

Repeated Reading

Research stresses the importance of practice in reading as a vehicle for achieving fluency. Guided reading and repeated oral reading activities significantly affect the development of fluency. Text used for repeated readings should be short (50–250 words long). Material should be at an easy level and become progressively more difficult as the student becomes more fluent.

Steps in Repeated Reading

The first reading is done with a fluent reader for comprehension and modeling. Students read a passage several times until they achieve fluency, defined by reading rate or word accuracy. Rereading increases word recognition and comprehension as well as fluency. To check student comprehension after each reading, ask a different question. Rereading is really about practicing reading text. Just as we become better runners when we run or better pianists when we play the piano, we become better readers when we read. Steps to use in repeated reading are listed below.

- Select or help the student to select text that is short (50–250 words, yet too long to memorize), from a story or passage that interests him or her.

- Explain that readings are timed and the student should focus on reading with speed and accuracy.

- Prepare a chart or graph for recording speed of reading and errors.

- The student reads to the teacher, parent, or tutor, who records the reading speed and number of errors on the graph. Talk about the text (for understanding) and any unknown words.

- Then have the student practice rereading the passage aloud as many times as he or she can. This can be done with a student partner or an adult, both in school and at home.

- For each successive reading, record the time. Students can see visible evidence of their progress.

- When the time goal (85 words per minute) is reached and reading is more expressive and fluid, move on to the next passage.

 Fluency

Generally, as reading speed increases, word recognition errors decrease. Repeated reading aids in sight word acquisition; it allows students to see the same words over and over again in print. Students transfer recognition of words from one situation to another. Material in anthologies and leveled reading books used for guided reading can be reread not only to improve sight vocabulary, but also to increase comprehension and build confidence. Remember to provide easy text for students needing fluency instruction. Students frustrated by unfamiliar vocabulary will not be anxious to read more.

Many genres work well for rereading—speeches, scripts (readers' theaters), plays, and songs all lend themselves well to repeated oral readings. Your music teacher may be able to suggest some songs for your class—lyrics are a form of poetry! Poetry is one of the best genres to use for repeated readings.

Poetry as a Vehicle for Repeated Reading

Reading poetry, written by the student or selected from a favorite poet, creates an authentic reason for reading a passage several times. Poetry is **meant to be shared orally** and performed for an audience. Unfortunately, poetry is one of the least studied genres in most language arts programs. For many teachers, focusing on proficiency skills in the fourth grade and meeting the demands for accountability preclude the creation of opportunities for the enjoyment of poetry. But poetry is an excellent vehicle for developing fluency.

Read your favorite poem aloud and use your voice to create mood, to connect **expression and meaning**, and to convey the **rhythm and rhyme** of the words. Become different characters as you read. Emphasize some words and whisper others, express the meaning with your pitch and tone, and project feeling into your delivery. Wasn't that easy? Wow! You just modeled fluent reading and made a huge connection with your students! See the checklist on page 27 and the activities on pages 28–36 for easy ways to include poetry activities into your day.

Name _____ Date _____

poetry, expression

Performing Poetry

For the Performer

Poem Name _____ Date _____

- ☐ Read the poem and identify unknown words.
- ☐ Read the poem again to find its meaning.
- ☐ Read a third time and look for clues in the text that tell you how to read it (repetition, punctuation).
- ☐ Practice reading the poem aloud.
- ☐ Rehearse the poem with a partner or fluent reader who can provide feedback. Your partner can use the checklist below to evaluate your performance.

....

For the Audience or Partner

Performer Name _____ Date _____

Poem Name _____

The performer understood the poem.

    yes   sometimes   no

The performer made the meaning clear to the audience.

    yes   sometimes   no

The performer read fluently, smoothly, and without hesitation.

    yes   sometimes   no

The performer used expression, intonation, and phrasing in his/her presentation.

    yes   sometimes   no

Published by Instructional Fair. Copyright protected.   0-7424-2824-9 *Reading for Every Child: Fluency*

Cleaning

1   Oh, how I HATE it!
2   Oh, what a CHORE!
3   Why can't I leave all of it
4   And just CLOSE THE DOOR?

5   It's taken me HOURS
6   And more—even DAYS of
7   Dumping and tossing in just
8   The right ways!
9   (To make it my own special place.)

10   Here's a sock, a shirt, my shoe,
11   CDs, games and toys (once new),
12   Scrunched chip bags, wrinkly wrappers from candy,
13   Old homework papers that MIGHT come in handy!

14   Dried-up markers and pencil stubs,
15   A collection of things from the past!
16   I am the artist who CREATED it ALL,
17   A treasure of things that will last!

18   And now I have to CLEAN IT UP?
19   Toss it, dust it, and more?
20   Why CAN'T I leave it alone—like it is,
21   And quietly just close my door?

 **Fluency**

Cleaning—Teacher Discussion Guide

After reading, ask questions about the poem. These can be used to generate discussion or prepared as a written activity. The following questions and activities require students to look at phrasing (chunking text), reading rate, and intonation.

1. Why did I read **hate**, **chore**, and **close the door** louder than the other words? How did the author tell me I needed to do that?

2. What about the exclamation marks—how did my voice change when I read those parts?

3. How did my voice sound when I read the last line?

4. In the second stanza, what happened when I came to the dash? Why did I do that?

5. When I came to the line in parentheses I lowered my voice. Why? Why did the author add line 9 and put it in parentheses?

6. In the third stanza, what did I do when I came to the commas? Why would I pause there?

7. Which words are hard for the class to read?

8. How did I make the words **scrunched** and **wrinkly** come alive in the third stanza? What did I do with my voice?

9. Who is the author? To whom is the author speaking in this poem? How does the author feel about cleaning?

10. How could we dramatize this poem? How many parts can we create?

11. What lines can we reread in a whisper? in a louder voice? Can we read this poem in a pleading voice? an angry voice? a frustrated voice?

12. Practice reading the poem over several times.

Name _____ Date _____

poetry, comprehension

Cleaning—Student Response Page

Directions: Use the poem "Cleaning" (page 28) to answer the questions below.

1. Explain who the speaker is in this poem and why you think so.

   _____
   _____
   _____

2. What argument is the speaker using to defend his or her position about cleaning?

   _____
   _____
   _____

3. What image do the words **scrunched** and **wrinkly** give you?

   a. creased   c. unsightly

   b. smooth   d. bulky

4. Use the back of this page to construct a web describing six things in your room. Use descriptive words to create a visual of the things you mention. For example, **ruffled lace pillow** or **cracked wooden bat**.

5. Respond to the speaker of the poem. Assume that you must persuade the speaker to clean the room. State three reasons for needing to do so.

   _____
   _____
   _____
   _____

Catch Up!?

1. Hurry! Rush! Move a little faster!
2. You're traveling much too slow!
3. I'll stop and wait, for just a bit,
4. But then I **really** have to go!
5. CATCH UP?

6. I pour it s- l- o- w- l- y, thick and red.
7. It flows around my fries,
8. And on my burger, sizzling hot,
9. It d- r- i- b- b- l- e- s down the sides.
10. KETCHUP!

Catch Up!?—Teacher Discussion Guide

Read the poem to the class to model expressive reading. Discuss the images students are creating in their minds as each stanza is read again. Then give each student a copy of the poem and display it on an overhead transparency. After reading, generate a discussion about the poem.

1. Discuss the way you read the poem and how the punctuation directed you to do so. Why is the word **really** in bold type? Why are **slowly** and **dribbles** written as they are?

2. Ask who the speaker is in the first stanza and to whom that person is speaking.

3. Where are they going? What is the rush all about?

4. How does the subject change in the second stanza? Is the speaker the same person who spoke in the first stanza?

5. What is the relationship between the words **catch up** and **ketchup**?

6. What was the author's purpose in writing this poem?

Practice reading the poem with the class in a variety of ways.

- Read the entire poem **chorally** with the class. Most readers will feel successful after several readings because of the support that reading together offers.

- Assign different lines to different students and try an **antiphonal reading**.

- Ask students to retell the story in each stanza in their own words. Doing so will indicate whether or not they understand the poem.

- Use the questions on page 33 to assess students' comprehension of the poem.

Name _____ Date_____

Fluency
poetry, comprehension

Catch Up!?—Student Response Page

Directions: Use the poem "Catch Up!?" (page 31) to answer the questions below.

1. Which word best describes the feelings of the speaker in the first stanza?

    a. thoughtful
    b. annoyed
    c. pensive

2. Do you think the speaker in the first stanza is the same person speaking in the second stanza? Explain your answer.

    _____

    _____

    _____

3. How would you describe the way the speaker in the second stanza feels?

    a. bashful
    b. curious
    c. excited

4. If you were reading this poem to a friend, what would you do when you saw the exclamation points in the first line?

    a. read louder
    b. read slower
    c. read with excitement

Published by Instructional Fair. Copyright protected. 0-7424-2824-9 *Reading for Every Child: Fluency*

The Perfect Meal

1 If I could design the perfect meal,
2 I'd make it such a tasty deal—
3 I'm not certain just what it might be,
4 But I promise you won't find **broccoli**!!!

5 No lima beans or succotash,
6 I assure you, no corned beef hash,
7 Doubtful on cucumbers or tomatoes,
8 And don't ask for any sweet potatoes!

9 I don't think I'll include broiled fish,
10 And no mushrooms in ANY dish!
11 No ham or turkey or pot roast,
12 No peppers, onions, or jelly toast!

13 I have a little sneaky hunch,
14 You won't find eggs at MY brunch!
15 Soup and salad aren't much of a winner,
16 So I doubt you'll find them at my dinner!

17 It's taking work, but still I strive
18 To include the food groups—aren't there five?
19 Fruits and veggies, protein too,
20 Some grains for carbs and a little moo—

21 The perfect meal! Did you guess?
22 It's really exquisite, I must confess …
23 If I had your number, I'd call on the phone,
24 It's a very berry peanut-popcorn ice cream cone!

The Perfect Meal—Teacher Discussion Guide

Read the poem aloud to your students. A good time to include poetry in your day is right as you transition to your language arts block. It gives students a fun way to shift gears and also allows you opportunities for repeated readings. Once students have heard the poem several times, concentrate a longer block of time discussing it with the following questions.

1. Who is the author of this poem? Is it an adult or a child? Does it have to be a child? Could it be someone who is eight? eighty?

2. What is the author's attitude toward ice cream? How do you know that?

3. How does the author feel about vegetables?

4. Why did the author put the word **broccoli** in bold type? What does that mean to you when you read aloud?

5. Why are the words **ANY** in line 10 and **MY** in line 14 written in capital letters? How would you indicate that to your audience when you read those words?

6. What is the rhyming pattern this author used?

7. Select two words that rhyme. How many other words can you think of that rhyme with them? How many rhyming word pairs can you find?

8. What is **brunch**?

9. If brunch is breakfast and lunch, what is lunch and dinner? What about breakfast and dinner?

10. Circle the contractions the author used in the poem. What two words did they each come from?

11. What do the dashes tell me to do when I read?

12. Is this a serious poem? What kind of tone did I use when I read it?

Published by Instructional Fair. Copyright protected.   0-7424-2824-9 *Reading for Every Child: Fluency*

Name _____ Date _____

poetry, partner reading

The Perfect Meal— Student Response Page

Directions: Use the poem "The Perfect Meal" (page 34) to do the activities below. You will need to find a partner to work with you.

1. Partners trade copies of the poem and take turns reading the poem to each other. The listener circles any words the reader doesn't know on the reader's copy of the poem.

2. After both partners have read, go back and look up the words you didn't know in the dictionary. Write the meanings near each word.

3. Circle all the places where you should pause when reading. Notice if the reader does that.

4. Listen for the reader's voice to go up when reading the questions in the last two stanzas.

5. Check the reader's reading rate for the first reading. Have the reader read again twice more and compare the rates for an increase in speed.

6. Read two lines to your partner and have him or her read the next two lines to you. Finish the poem this way. Then switch who starts.

7. Read alternate lines with your partner.

8. Tape-record one stanza as you read. Listen to it and talk with your partner about how you read it. Then let your partner record a stanza.

9. Write the last two lines over and change them to include your favorite food. Make an illustration to go with it.

10. Read the poem with another pair of partners. You can:
    - echo read
    - read alternate stanzas
    - read alternate lines
    - read chorally (in unison)
    - read antiphonally (different lines for each student)

Published by Instructional Fair. Copyright protected.

0-7424-2824-9 Reading for Every Child: Fluency

Fluency

Expressive Reading

Less fluent readers read in a choppy word-by-word manner. Reading with expression incorporates **prosody**—pitch, intonation, stress, emphasis, rate, rhythm, and appropriate phrasing. Fluent readers who incorporate these elements into their reading provide evidence of their comprehension of a text.

It's All About Emphasis

Read these three examples of the same sentence with emphasis on three different words:

- **She** wore her blue shoes to work.   (catty?)
- She wore her **blue** shoes to work.   (outrageous?)
- She wore her blue shoes to **work**.   (inappropriate?)

Notice the subtle changes in meaning when the stress is placed on different words. Try these sentences:

- **His** report was so boring.   (focus on him)
- His report was so **boring**.   (emphasis is now on the report)

Meaning can also change depending punctuation and where the reader pauses. See these two sentences:

- Woman—without her, man is nothing.
- Woman—without her man, is nothing.

The meaning depends on where you pause, doesn't it? These sentences are open to some controversy, so I'll leave the interpretation up to you! Students can learn strategies for expressive reading. Some ideas are listed on the next page.

Fluency

Strategies for Expressive Reading

- Begin a sentence with a bit higher pitch than you use to end it.
- Raise your voice at the end of a question.
- Bring your voice straight up for an exclamation.
- Pause at a comma.
- Pause longer at a period.
- If there is dialogue, the character speaks in a higher pitch than the narrator.
- If there is a key word, raise your voice or stretch it out for emphasis. The audience can pick up the importance of that word in this way.
- Change rhythm—speed up and slow down.
- Change tone—use a warm voice, a sad voice, an angry or excited voice.

Matching facial expression and body language to the words in a sentence shows that the reader comprehends the meaning of those words. Oral expression conveys comprehension of the text. Before television when a radio performance was given, the audience relied on the speaker to read expressively to convey meaning. And it worked! You can access recordings of old radio programs at Internet Web sites if you want to hear an authentic piece like "The Shadow," "CBS Radio Mystery Theater," or Lucille Ball's radio broadcasts. You can also get your own copies of recordings from a local library or bookstore if you'd like to play them in your classroom. Another option is to listen to a sporting event being broadcast on the radio to experience meaning conveyed through expressive verbal communication.

Practice expressive reading with your students by:

- choral reading
- echo reading
- modeling reading
- performing readers' theaters

Fluency

Classroom Activities for Expressive Reading

- Discuss the importance of expressive reading.
- Brainstorm the different kinds of emotions we can portray and put them on a semantic web.
- Explain that when we read orally, we convey the emotions the author wants us to feel.
- Review the punctuation marks writers use and how readers change the tone, volume, rhythm, and pitch of their voices when those marks direct their reading.
- Select a text passage you want to read. Make a copy of it and use correction fluid to cover the punctuation marks. Then make copies for the class.
    - Have students insert the correct punctuation marks on their copy of the text as you read.
    - Put the text passage on an overhead projector when you finish reading and ask the students how they marked the sentences in the passage.

Activities with a Partner

- Students should select partners and read the passage to each other.
- The teacher selects examples of sentences ending with periods, question marks, or exclamation points. Find others containing commas that chunk words into phrases.
- Copy the sentences on strips of paper and pass them out to students in pairs so that each student has several different sentences.
- The reading partner reads a sentence and the listener has to identify the punctuation mark that was used in that sentence based on the partner's oral reading. Partners take turns reading to each other until all sentences have been read.
- Have students then write and punctuate three sentences of their own.
- Repeat the activity with student sentences.

expression—nonfiction

It's a Bird! It's a Plane! It's a ... Penguin?

1   Did you ever wonder if penguins can fly?

2   Have you ever seen one flying?

3   Long ago, penguins' ancestors were indeed birds that could fly, but they lost their ability to do so as they evolved.

4   There aren't many large predators of penguins in the Antarctic.

5   There is little need for penguins to fly away to escape an enemy.

6   Instead, penguins are excellent divers!

7   Birds that fly have hollow bones and minimal weight.

8   Birds that dive have solid bones and higher weight, and this is true of penguins.

9   Penguins can access food sources unavailable to other birds that are not as adept at diving.

10 Penguins can dive as deep as a thousand meters and remain under water for up to twenty minutes!

11 Even though you will never see a penguin fly through the air, you just might see one "flying" through the water.

Fluency

It's a Bird! It's a Plane! It's a ... Penguin?— Teacher Discussion Guide

Read the passage to the class, modeling expressive reading. Give the students copies of the passage to follow as you read it again. Then generate discussion questions such as the following.

1. What do you think the author wants us to do when we read the title? What do the ellipses (three dots) tell us to do? What kind of expression would you use—surprise? amazement?

2. How did my voice sound at the end of the first two sentences? Why did it sound that way?

3. What did I do after I read the word **fly** in sentence 3? What did that tell the listener about the text?

4. When I read sentences 7 and 8, how did I indicate with my voice that a period was at the end of the sentences?

5. What word would you read a little louder in sentence 9? The word is **not**. Why would you emphasize that word?

6. How did I read sentence 10? Why did the author end it with an exclamation mark?

An extension activity can be added by:

- having students write a brief summary statement in their own words.
- having students compare two ways birds that fly differ from penguins.
- having partners research another penguin fact and write a paragraph to read orally to the class. You might compile a list of questions they can choose from such as:
    - Why do penguins have white fronts and black backs?
    - How do penguins sleep?
    - Do penguins have feathers?
    - Do penguins "talk"?
    - How do penguins give birth to their offspring?

Published by Instructional Fair. Copyright protected.   0-7424-2824-9 *Reading for Every Child: Fluency*

Name _____ Date _____

Fluency — expression—nonfiction, comprehension

It's a Bird! It's a Plane! It's a ... Penguin?— Student Response Guide

Directions: Refer to the passage on page 40 to answer the following questions.

1. Which sentence best summarizes the main idea of the passage?

    a. Penguins are too lazy to fly.
    b. Penguins lost their ability to fly through evolution.
    c. Penguins are able to fly, but they would rather dive.

2. Penguins are birds that—

    a. dive farther than other birds to access food.
    b. don't weigh very much.
    c. are not able to remain under water for more than five minutes.

3. One thing this paragraph did not tell us is—

    a. how far penguins dive down in the water.
    b. whether penguins have solid bones or hollow bones.
    c. what the penguin's predators are.

4. If you were monitoring your partner's fluency in reading this paragraph, you would check for—

    a. reading speed.
    b. spelling accuracy.
    c. legibility.

Published by Instructional Fair. Copyright protected.　　0-7424-2824-9 *Reading for Every Child: Fluency*

Fluency

Readers' Theater

One of the most fabulous strategies for rereading text and practicing expressive reading is readers' theater. Readers' theater provides an authentic reason to reread text and is an excellent way of engaging students in fluency practice.

In readers' theater, students read from scripts that they hold during the performance. Parts are not memorized. There are no stage sets, props, or costumes. Characters can be identified with name tags that the students wear if you wish to do so. Narration frames the presentation. All students can participate and be successful. Readers' theater:

- allows students to express themselves creatively.
- improves oral reading fluency.
- improves comprehension through interpretation.
- engages performers and the audience in active listening.
- promotes cooperative learning.
- creates an avenue for enjoying literature.
- is an authentic strategy for rereading.
- is an instructional activity.
- provides opportunities for modeling and feedback.
- is tremendously enjoyable.
- encourages speaking to an audience.
- promotes word recognition.
- supports less fluent readers as they read with more fluent readers.

Students should read text at their independent or instructional level. Scripts can be fictional works, poetry, speeches, or nonfiction; a variety of scripts can be accessed on the Internet or purchased in commercially prepared books. If you want to get really creative, write your own script based on a trade book, fairy tale, or content-area text or write an original script with your class.

Fluency

The key to a successful experience is practice, practice, practice in school and at home. Students need to practice until they can read their parts fluently. Reluctant readers must have opportunities to become comfortable with their parts and with reading in front of others. Shy students become more outgoing and confident; less inhibited students will love the chance to participate in appropriate classroom drama! When students practice, they need to remember that a successful, meaningful performance depends on their appropriate **expressive reading**. The audience is imagining the setting and most of the action from the reader's interpretation and oral delivery of the story.

Getting into Character—Role-Playing (A Character Puzzle)

A fun way to practice character before working on your readers' theater is to practice role-playing. Gather the reading materials listed in the first column below, or use others you have on hand. Students create characters by selecting one element from each of the categories. For example, if a student picks **travel brochure, wistful,** and **teacher**, he or she has to read a travel brochure playing the role of a wistful teacher—perhaps one longing to be on a sunny beach someplace! Ask students to think about how that would sound and why it would sound that way.

Material	Emotion	Character
recipe	angry	bus driver
phone book	wistful	salesperson
sports page article	discouraged	reporter
how-to instructions	annoyed	chef
driving directions	amused	announcer
help wanted ad	confident	recruiter
classified ad	enthusiastic	applicant
news headline	excited	travel agent
travel brochure	confused	teacher

Fluency

Model by doing the activity yourself first. Ask the students to pick something from each list before you tell them what you are going to do. Then tell them what the task is and ask for their input as you prepare your presentation by thinking aloud. Finally, model how you decide how your reading should sound and how you practice your expressive reading before your presentation.

After you read, discuss what students think was good or what they would have changed. Students can pull out sentences they want to try reading orally so they can get into the role of the character as they see it. Partners can then try the formula with a new selection and prepare to present it.

Getting Started with Readers' Theaters

Select a script for your students. Model fluent reading of the script by reading it to them first. Then discuss the script as you would when conducting a guided reading lesson to ensure understanding of the setting, character traits, and roles in the story and the main idea of the plot. Here are some suggestions to help you get started.

1. Make a copy of the script for each student.

2. Have students highlight (in yellow) their own parts (assigned by the teacher or selected by the student).

3. Mark any stage directions with another color highlighter.

4. Read the script together (choral reading).

5. Students read over their parts silently. Students circle words they don't know and find the meanings.

6. Students begin to read their parts aloud. Discuss their characters with them and consider:

    - How does my character feel?
    - How would my character sound?
    - How should I adjust my voice for expressive reading?
    - How would my character look (facial expression and actions)?

7. Point out the differences between characters and narrators. Characters usually speak in a higher pitch than narrators.

Fluency

8. Rehearse the script many times! Do this with all of the participants present.

   - Readers should look at the audience or other characters (as indicated by the script) as well as the script.
   - Remind readers to speak slowly and loudly.
   - Encourage students to have fun! This is the time to act and bring some drama to the story!
   - Practice giving time to transition between characters and the narrator when speaking.
   - Have students practice at home with family members taking on other parts.
   - Practice parts with partners and share positive feedback.

9. Performance is the final step. Be as encouraging as you can and things will fall into place—somehow!

   - Remind students not to look if someone enters the room. However, if an announcement is made, stop until it is over.
   - If a reader makes a mistake, it's okay to start over or keep on going and pretend it was right.
   - If someone forgets to read his or her part, either skip it or have the next reader read it. Don't call out names to remind students to read!
   - Readers can sit or stand anywhere in the room. A variation is to have readers surround the audience members, who are seated in the middle of the room.

10. Housekeeping tips:

    - One way to group students is by guided-reading groups, but if you want to group by mixed levels, that's fine too.
    - Students can select scripts from several you have chosen.
    - Try to tie a script into a story or a topic you are studying or that is part of a content-area lesson.
    - After students become familiar with the readers' theater genre, have them try writing their own scripts.

The Great Cake Taker
Based on a story by Susan J. Herron

Cast of Characters
NARRATOR 1
NARRATOR 2
NARRATOR 3
NARRATOR 4
NARRATOR 5
BOY
GIRL
POLICE CHIEF
MAYOR
CROWD

NARRATOR 1   Everybody loves a birthday and—

NARRATOR 2   —what's a birthday without a cake?

NARRATOR 3   After all, you need a place to put the candles!

NARRATOR 1   As I was saying before I was—

NARRATOR 2   —so rudely interrupted!

NARRATOR 4   There's a story in here somewhere. Shall we begin?

NARRATOR 3	Oh, I just love the "once upon a times"! Is it one of those?
NARRATOR 1	ONCE UPON A TIME, in a small town there was a—
NARRATOR 5	*(interrupting)* —a TERRIBLE problem. AWFUL, JUST THE PITS!
NARRATOR 1	It happened every time one of the children had a birthday.
NARRATOR 3	Just before it was time for cake and ice cream,
NARRATOR 5	no matter how well the cake was guarded or how carefully it was hidden away …
NARRATOR 4	it disappeared!
NARRATOR 2	Yep—every time! Never failed!
NARRATOR 3	It's not a lie, I tell you!
BOY	I can testify to that—I never had a cake until I was in my late twenties!
NARRATOR 1	*(glaring at boy)* Ah-hum! We seem to be getting ahead of ourselves.
BOY	*(apologetic)* Sorry!
NARRATOR 1	Once in a great while,
NARRATOR 3	once in a blue moon,
NARRATOR 1	a few crumbs might be left behind, but—
NARRATOR 4	—no one wanted to eat them.

Name _____ **Date** _____

Fluency
readers' theater

NARRATOR 5	Now it might surprise you to know that the people in this town KNEW what was happening!
CROWD	They really did KNOW???
GIRL	*(nodding)* Yep!
NARRATOR 2	Seems like, out of the hills just behind the town there was a fella coming down and—
NARRATOR 3	—he was known as THE GREAT CAKE TAKER!
CROWD	*(frightened)* Ooooooh!
NARRATOR 5	He could feel when those cakes were coming.
BOY AND GIRL	He knew! HE KNEW!!!
NARRATOR 4	And then when the smell wafted up into those hills—
GIRL AND BOY	—well, he never missed one!
CROWD	*(amazed)* NOT EVEN ONE?
NARRATOR 1	Now this is what he looked like:
BOY	He was GREAT BIG and HUGE and
GIRL	GIGANTIC!
BOY	And his whole body was covered with green fur!

Published by Instructional Fair. Copyright protected.　　49　　0-7424-2824-9 *Reading for Every Child: Fluency*

NARRATOR 3	Green as grass I tell you!
NARRATOR 5	And his legs were real skinny.
GIRL	And he had a head as round as the moon,
NARRATOR 2	with one yellow eye like a lemon and the other one was—
NARRATOR 4	—red like a ripe tomato!
NARRATOR 1	His eyebrows (well, if you must know it was truly just ONE eyebrow!) were all thick and black and shaggy.
NARRATOR 3	*(disgusted)* You'd think he'd know something about grooming!
BOY	And his nose was all squashed all over his face like a smashed up—
GIRL	—jack-o-lantern on Halloween.
NARRATOR 5	And he had little purple bumps all over his face.
NARRATOR 1	I told you he wasn't very tidy.
NARRATOR 2	When he smiled—which was only on other people's birthdays, if you know what I mean—
NARRATOR 3	—his one jagged greenish, yellowish, brownish tooth showed right on top!
CROWD	*(grossed out)* NASTY!!!
BOY	Did you mention his ears?

GIRL	YUCK! Tiny, too small for THAT head, and all pointed, too!
NARRATOR 4	The townspeople decided to have a meeting to see what to do about this ongoing problem.
NARRATOR 1	You can tell that they didn't make any spontaneous decisions in this neck of the woods.
NARRATOR 2	The mayor shouted,
MAYOR	*(loudly)* "There will be a $1,000 reward!"
NARRATOR 3	His brother-in-law, the police chief, roared,
POLICE CHIEF	*(determined)* "I vow I'll get him this time!"
CROWD	*(hopeful, but uncertain)* Uh-huh!
NARRATOR 3	But no one knew how. No one—except little Dougie Walters.
MAYOR	Just imagine! Dougie, only seven years old, says *(barely in a whisper)*,
POLICE CHIEF	*(talking in a little-boy voice)* "I think the Cake Taker is lonely. We should have a birthday party just for him."
MAYOR	*(thoughtful)* "Well, well,"
BOY	said the mayor.

POLICE CHIEF	*(considering)* "Hmmmmm,"
GIRL	said the police chief.
CROWD	*(enthusiastic)* "Hooray for Dougie!" shouted all the people.
NARRATOR 1	The following Sunday everyone in town gathered in the town square.
NARRATOR 2	The town hall was decorated with streamers and balloons of every color, size, and shape!
NARRATOR 3	The town band was dressed in full uniform and ready to march.
NARRATOR 4	And in the middle of it all—
NARRATOR 5	—was a birthday cake like no other!
MAYOR	It had seventeen layers of delicious, delectable cake in—
POLICE CHIEF	*(remembering, licking lips)* chocolate, banana, spice, white, and even strawberry!
BOY	And the icing looked like swirls of creamy peaks of marshmallows—
GIRL	—with jellybeans, and chocolate pieces, and bits of red licorice tucked in.
NARRATOR 2	There were yellow flowers with bright green leaves and blue icing letters that spelled out—
NARRATOR 3	HAPPY BIRTHDAY, GREAT CAKE TAKER!!!
NARRATOR 4	And one hundred candles glowing on top—

Fluency

readers' theater

NARRATOR 5	—of it all!
MAYOR	Everyone in the town was there waiting, and—
POLICE CHIEF	—waiting, and
MAYOR	*(building suspense)* —waiting.
POLICE CHIEF	They waited more—
BOY	*(impatiently)* —and more.
GIRL	From far away you could hear, THUD—THUD—THUD!
MAYOR	And very slowly but steadily, the Great Cake Taker came down from the hills.
POLICE CHIEF	He looked.
BOY	The people looked back.
GIRL	He looked.
BOY	They looked.
GIRL	He smiled.
BOY	They smiled.
NARRATOR 1	Little Dougie walked forward, climbed a ladder up to the top of the cake, and lit the candles.
NARRATOR 2	All one hundred.
NARRATOR 3	Everyone sang "HAPPY BIRTHDAY TO YOU!! HAPPY BIRTHDAY, DEAR GREAT, HAPPY BIRTHDAY TO YOU!"

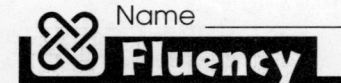

NARRATOR 4	Then the cake was cut—I'm not sure how, but I'm just telling this story, not living it—and the finest party in the history of the town was underway!
NARRATOR 5	There was music and dancing and singing!
MAYOR	Even fireworks for the celebration!
POLICE CHIEF	To this day, in that town, no child has ever lost a birthday cake.
BOY	Thanks to little Dougie—
GIRL	kids can just share cake with their friends!!
CROWD	Hooray!

THE END

Fluency

The Great Cake Taker—Teacher Activity Guide

You've completed a successful readers' theater performance with your class. Now what? Below are some ideas for in-class activities and ways to give students a chance to evaluate their performance.

Activities for After the Performance

- The class can perform the script for younger students. After the performance, slowly reread the description of the Cake Taker in sequential order so the younger students can draw him from the description. Allow them to talk about the pictures and their favorite part of the story.

- Ask your students what inferences they can make about the Cake Taker. What motivated him to behave the way he did?

- What do your students think of Dougie's solution? Ask them to write alternate solutions and present them orally to the class.

- Talk about the author's purpose. Was it to entertain, inform, persuade, or express an opinion?

- Make a cake and let the students decorate it to celebrate a job well done!

Evaluation

Students will know if they are pleased with a performance. Readers have worked hard to become more fluent and to convey the story through oral interpretation. They are storytellers portraying characters, relaying events and emotions to the audience. Positive feedback from their peers should be given after a performance. Self-evaluation or group evaluation can be accomplished by using the form on the next page.

| Name _____ | Date _____ |

Fluency   readers' theater

Student Evaluation Form for Readers' Theater

Directions: Use this form to assess how well you and your classmates did performing your readers' theater.

Name of Script _____

Date of Performance _____

1. I read my lines at an appropriate speed—not too fast, not too slow.

    yes   sometimes   no

2. My voice was loud enough for people to hear me.

    yes   sometimes   no

3. I said my lines with expression so people could understand my character.

    yes   sometimes   no

4. The audience liked the performance.

    yes   sometimes   no

5. The best thing about doing the readers' theater was . . .

    _____

6. The worst thing about doing the readers' theater was . . .

    _____

Fluency

Partner Reading

Repeated oral reading with feedback is one of the best ways to increase fluency. However, repeated readings of a text require a lot of time that teachers feel they don't have. This makes partner reading a valuable tool.

Supported Reading

Partner reading is a supported reading activity where paired students take turns reading aloud to each other. The stronger reader reads first, modeling fluent reading. Pairs can consist of teacher and student, student and student, parent and student, older child and younger child, or tutor and student. Partnerships can be created in several ways:

- fluent reader with less fluent reader
- self-selected partners
- leveled pairs of readers
- student-adult partners

The more fluent reader demonstrates reading and provides support during reading. He or she can read first, then the less fluent reader reads the same paragraph or page aloud. At this time, the more fluent reader assists with word recognition, phrasing, and reading with expression as needed. Reading can also be done aloud simultaneously (choral reading). The less fluent partner rereads until he or she can read the passage independently.

Students can select text at their instructional or independent level. This is not a time to create more challenges with text that is sure to be too difficult. Stronger readers should read at a rate comfortable for the less fluent readers. If the less fluent readers feel ready, they can signal that they want to go on alone. Support readers either read along in a whisper or become silent. When readers require help, they can indicate that help is needed.

Fluency

Students reading with partners can sit side by side facing the same direction or face to face looking at each other. Some of the strategies partners can use are listed below.

- Engage in choral reading with one copy of the book for two readers (or with each reader having a copy of the book).
- Echo reading—one partner reads first, then the other reads the same text again (a sentence or a longer section of text can be read).
- Record your reading of a passage (individually or together), and then play it back. Discuss how the reading sounds.
- Share parts in a story (you be this character, and I'll be that one).
- Take turns reading one or several pages.
- Read silently first, then aloud.
- Take turns retelling the passage to each other.

When students partner with adults for reading, the adult reads first, and then the student reads. The adult provides assistance and encouragement. After about three rereadings, the student should be able to read the text independently and fluently.

Shared Reading

Another variation of partner reading is shared reading. The teacher (tutor, parent, or other fluent reader) first reads a text to the student. Next, the student reads the text with the fluent reader (both reading aloud at the same time). Then the student reads the text to the fluent reader (student reading out loud alone). Finally, the student and fluent reader return to the text several times to reread it. The rereading is accompanied by discussion of the text and completion of extension activities designed by the teacher.

There are many books designed for two or more readers. See the resources section beginning on page 77 for suggestions. Poems can be great fun to read with a partner. The poem on the next page is a good one to get you started.

Invisible

1   Did you ever wonder how it would be
2   If you could be *anywhere*, but no one could see
3   **You?**

4   I would know everything Franny whispered to Fred
5   And repeat every word about Nathan she said . . .
6   **Imagine!**

7   At lunch, you could swear your pizza was here,
8   But two seconds later it might disappear—
9   **Where?**

10   If my mom does the wash, do you think she will stare
11   As she feels a breeze when the underwear
12   **Flies?**

13   Would my dad shake his head if he didn't know
14   Why the stations kept changing on the radio?
15   **Curious!**

16   Did you ever wonder how it might be
17   If you could be *anywhere*, but no one could see,
18   **YOU?**

Fluency

Invisible—Teacher Discussion Guide

First, read the poem on page 59 to the class, modeling expressive reading. Pass out copies of the poem so students can follow the text as you read it again. They can highlight punctuation or make notes as you read. Then discuss the following questions.

1. Who do you think the speaker in this poem is? Why do you think so?

2. What is the speaker's attitude about being invisible? How do you know that?

3. Why is the last word in each stanza **bold**? How does that direct my reading of that word?

4. Which lines would I read with my voice elevated at the end of the line?

5. How could you vary the reading of the last word? (louder, whispered, read by another voice)

6. Where would I pause in my reading?

7. Is the speaker speaking to anyone? Who? (us, a friend, the mirror?)

8. Try this to accentuate the **rhythm** of language. Put the poem to a beat by having student partners tap/clap this beat as they read, so the tapping accentuates the rhythm of the words.

Example:

First reader:	"Did you ever wonder" *(tap, tap, clap)*
Second reader:	"Did you ever wonder" *(tap, tap, clap)*
First partner:	"how it would be" *(tap, tap, clap)*
Second reader:	"how it would be" *(tap, tap, clap)*

Published by Instructional Fair. Copyright protected.

0-7424-2824-9 *Reading for Every Child: Fluency*

Name _____ Date_____

Fluency

partner reading, poetry

Invisible—Student Response Sheet

Directions: Find a partner and use the poem on page 59 to do the following activities.

1. Take turns reading the entire poem to each other.

2. Read alternating lines.

3. One partner reads two lines and the other reads the bold word.

4. Read the poem quickly. Then read the poem slowly.

5. Time your partner's reading rate for three separate readings over three days. Use the chart below to record your results.

6. Read the poem together at the same time (choral reading).

7. Read the poem in a whisper as if it were a secret.

8. Read the poem as if you were trying to be sneaky!

Name of Poem _____

Total Number of Words _____

Reading	Date	Time (in minutes)
1		
2		
3		

Published by Instructional Fair. Copyright protected.

0-7424-2824-9 *Reading for Every Child: Fluency*

Fluency

Fluency Development Lesson

This fluency development lesson can be used as an intervention strategy with the whole class. It was developed by Rasinski, Padak, Linek, and Sturtevant ("Effects of Fluency Development on Urban Second-Grade Readers," *Journal of Educational Research*, 87:158–165). The lesson targets rate, accuracy, expressive reading, and comprehension. Materials used can be short (50–150 words) selections from trade books, basal text, anthologies, poems, and riddles. The goal of the lesson is to increase both prosody and automaticity through repeated readings.

The steps in the lesson are as follows:

- The teacher reads the text aloud to the class, modeling expressive reading.

- The text is discussed to be sure that students understand its meaning.

- The class reads the text chorally. Each student has his or her own copy of the text.

- Students then pair up to read the text to each other. Each partner reads the text three times.

- Students are encouraged to practice reading at home to maximize opportunities to build fluency.

- Students can read the text aloud for the class if they wish to perform. They can do so as individuals, with a partner, or in a small group.

You can extend the lesson by focusing on particular vocabulary within the text. Target these words when you are discussing comprehension. The more exposure students have to unfamiliar words, the more likely those words will become part of their usable vocabulary. The more often students read a passage with understanding, the more confident they will become in their ability to be fluent readers.

Bubble, Bubble, Toil and Trouble

"**Eeek**!" came a scream from the kitchen.

"What's going on here?" gasped Brandon as he breathlessly arrived on the scene.

"Help me!" shrieked Megan. "It won't stop! It just gets bigger and bigger and—"

"Slow down, Meg! You're running around like a maniac!"

"Can't you see it?" Megan yelled. "Look! The dishwasher! Bubbles—everywhere—the FLOOR!!!"

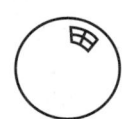

"**WOW**! Did you—?" Brandon's voice trailed off.

"Did I what?" questioned Megan.

"Tell me!" demanded Brandon.

"Mom just asked me to run the dishwasher, that's all. So I poured the soap in!" Megan explained.

"How much did you put in?" asked Brandon.

"I don't know—maybe a cup like Mom uses when she does the laundry," said Megan.

"**The laundry**!" shouted Brandon. "The laundry?! This is **NOT** the laundry!"

"I know," Megan responded meekly. "Can you help me? We can put water in there and—"

"**Water? Are you crazy?** If we add water to soap we only get more—"

"Bubbles?" said Megan gloomily.

"**Bubbles!**" exclaimed Brandon firmly. "When will mom be back?"

"I'm not sure," answered Megan.

Usually Brandon was a walking encyclopedia of information, so Megan was really counting on him to save the day!

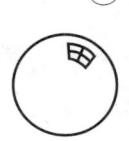

Fluency

Bubble, Bubble, Toil and Trouble—Teacher Discussion Guide

Use the story on page 63 to frame a fluency development lesson. Whether you are targeting specific students who need intervention or working as a class to develop fluency skills, this story works well for oral reading activities. First, read the passage to your students, modeling expressive reading. Then discuss the meaning of the passage, focusing on both vocabulary and comprehension. Use the questions below to guide your discussion. Follow this with repeated readings, having students pair up with partners (see page 65).

1. Find as many words as you can that describe characters' feelings. List them. Which ones are verbs? Which ones are adverbs?

2. Look at the words written in bold print. Explain why each of them is written that way.

3. Find the words written in capital letters. Explain why the author wrote them that way.

4. What do you think the relationship is between Brandon and Megan? How do you know that?

5. In your own words, describe how Megan is feeling.

6. What words would describe how Brandon is feeling?

7. How does the author want you to read dialogue ending with an exclamation mark? What does that mark convey to the reader?

8. Why does the author use dashes? What direction does that give the reader?

9. Describe the visual images you have from reading this selection. How would you draw what you see in your mind?

10. Who do you predict will be the hero in this story? Why do you think so?

Published by Instructional Fair. Copyright protected. 0-7424-2824-9 Reading for Every Child: Fluency

Name _____ Date_____
Fluency
fluency development—fiction

Bubble, Bubble, Toil and Trouble—Student Response Page

Directions: Use the story on page 63 to answer the questions below. You will need to work with a partner.

1. Practice "talking the talk." That is, how would Megan and Brandon actually sound if you overheard their conversation? Pick one line to read to your partner, and then your partner can read one to you. Read until you have completed the selection.

2. List six emotions you have felt from time to time. Choose three. Then write a sentence to show that emotion and read it to your partner. See if your partner can guess what emotion it is from your expressive reading.

3. Write the three emotions you chose and the three your partner chose on separate cards (six cards). Record yourselves saying the sentences you and your partner wrote. Play the recording for another pair of partners and see if they can pick the card with the emotion you are expressing.

4. Choose three of the verbs from the selection (**questioned, demanded, gasped, shrieked,** and so on). Write a new sentence in which someone says something to express that same emotion.

5. Draw a picture of the scenario described in "Bubble, Bubble, Toil and Trouble" with your partner. Talk about what you are including in your picture and why.

6. With your partner, predict what will happen next and write an ending for the story.

7. Think of a time you were involved in a "disaster" and write about what happened, who was there with you, where you were, and how you resolved the situation.

Published by Instructional Fair. Copyright protected. 0-7424-2824-9 *Reading for Every Child: Fluency*

Washington and Lincoln

Every year in February, on the Monday between Abraham Lincoln's birthday (February 12) and George Washington's birthday (February 22), we celebrate Presidents' Day to honor these great leaders. Federal offices close, so there is no mail delivery and no school for most of us. Washington was the first president of the United States and Lincoln led our country through the Civil War. Legends are often repeated along with the facts about great historical figures, and Washington and Lincoln are no exception.

Legend has it that when George was about six years old, he received his very own hatchet! He was quite fond of it and set out to try it out in his family's garden. George's father was very proud of a young cherry tree he had planted, and, as luck would have it, George swung his hatchet into the tree and nicked the bark. Sadly, the tree later died. When George's father discovered the cuts on the tree, he quickly returned to the house and demanded to know who had cut into the bark. Brave little George started to cry and replied, "I cannot tell a lie father! I did it with my hatchet." George's father was not angry and did not punish George because he had told the truth.

In contrast to the legend of the cherry tree, which has never been proven, we know that Abraham Lincoln truly was worthy of the nickname "Honest Abe." Before becoming president, Lincoln was a lawyer for twenty years. He was not a very financially successful lawyer. However, there are many documented examples of his honesty. Lincoln didn't like to charge people who were poor, as he was, for his services. Once, a client sent him a payment of twenty-five dollars, and Lincoln sent ten dollars back to him. Sometimes Lincoln encouraged his clients to settle their disputes out of court to save them money. Of course, then he didn't get paid at all! Lincoln didn't value money as much as he valued honesty and decency and caring about other people.

Fluency

Washington and Lincoln—Teacher Discussion Guide

Use the passage on page 66 to frame a fluency development lesson. Follow the steps below to lead your students through modeled reading, comprehension, and various ways to engage in repeated readings.

1. Begin by putting the names of George Washington and Abraham Lincoln on two separate webs. Ask students to tell you what they know about these two men. Use overhead transparencies or large chart paper so everyone can see the information.

2. Read the selection to the class, modeling fluent reading. Be sure everyone has a copy of the text.

3. After reading, ask students to tell you the big ideas (main idea, key facts) from the selection. Discuss the theme and meaning of the passage (honesty and integrity).

4. To foster comprehension, discuss the meaning of the following words.

legend	**client**
fond	**dispute**
nicked	**worthy**

5. Reread the selection with a whole-class choral reading.

6. After the choral reading, ask: What did we do when we came to an exclamation point? Why did we do that? Can you find an example and read that sentence aloud?

7. Read the lines where young George responds to his father as if you were a six-year-old boy.

8. Have students practice reading with a partner. Assign the first two paragraphs to one student and the next two to the other. After reading aloud, the reader has to turn the selection over and retell as much as he or she can without looking back at the text. The listening partner can check back in the text and give feedback when the reader is finished. Then partners change roles.

Name _____   Date _____

Fluency   fluency development—nonfiction

Washington and Lincoln— Student Response Page

Directions: Refer to the passage on page 66 to answer the following questions.

1. What was the author's purpose in writing this selection?

    a. to entertain
    b. to persuade
    c. to inform

2. Which proverb best applies to this entire selection?

    a. Honesty is the best policy.
    b. A friend in need is a friend indeed.
    c. You can't tell a book by its cover.

3. If you could interview either one of these two men, whom would you pick and what would you ask him?

    _____
    _____

4. Think of a time that you were honest and told the truth even though you didn't know what the consequences would be. Write about it and include who, what, when, where, and describe the end result.

    _____
    _____

5. Do you have a nickname? If so, what is it and how did you get it? If not, choose one and tell why you picked it for yourself.

    _____
    _____

Published by Instructional Fair. Copyright protected.   0-7424-2824-9 Reading for Every Child: Fluency

Fluency

Comprehension

Imagine I give you a manual to build the engine for your car. You're a good reader. Can you do it? If you don't have the background knowledge and technical vocabulary you need and are unable to make connections with the concepts in the text, I'll most likely see you looking confused and bewildered. And if I see that, even after you were able to read the manual with great fluency, I will know you didn't "get it." That's how it is with student reading comprehension. The ability to read something does not necessarily mean students have understood it.

Comprehension is the goal of reading; fluent readers not only read with appropriate pace and expression, but also **with understanding**. Fluent readers are recognizing words and comprehending at the same time. Less fluent readers are so busy decoding words that they lose the meaning of them and comprehension is compromised. Some students may recognize words in isolation, but are unable to read them fluently in text.

What Does Comprehension Look Like?

You can't see comprehension going on because it takes place in the reader's mind, but nonetheless you will know who got it and who didn't. Reading comprehension requires the reader to actively construct meaning from print. It is the reader who makes text meaningful by activating his or her background experiences and knowledge. Readers who comprehend text use strategies such as predicting, decoding, summarizing, analyzing, questioning, reflecting, and monitoring understanding. Good readers do these things automatically. They are not aware of using the strategies while they are reading.

The next page lists two ways you can help your students develop their comprehension as they work to become fluent readers. Literature circles allow students to draw on the strengths of various group members as they discuss a text. Once all members are confident with the passage, you can have each one perform an oral retelling as a way of evaluating comprehension.

Fluency

Literature Circles

Literature circles give students many opportunities to read aloud and discuss meaning. The more students read the passage, the more they comprehend. Students take responsibility for reading, discussing, and evaluating literature in a cooperative group setting. You will guide, monitor, support, and observe. In the beginning, you will demonstrate the roles each group member will assume. The roles are listed below.

Passage Picker. Locates passages to read aloud and discuss.

Artful Artist. Draws a picture related to the reading.

Connector. Finds connections between the book and the world you know.

Word Wizard. Selects puzzling, interesting, or unfamiliar words in the selection.

Discussion Director. Develops a list of questions the group might discuss.

There are variations on the names of the roles, but the basic idea is the same. Later on, the group needs to become more independent of you and learn to rely on each other for their learning. When organizing literature circles, you can keep the groups organized by reading level, or try mixed grouping to give peer support for struggling readers. To begin literature circles with a shorter text, try the story on pages 73–74.

Oral Retellings

A retelling allows you to look at a student's ability to construct meaning, make inferences, organize information, and summarize texts. Oral retellings are a great way to develop and assess fluency. In a retelling, a student tells the story again, recounting main ideas and supporting details. The retelling is told in his or her own words and not copied from the text. No new details are added. Events are related in sequence.

You can use one of the rubrics on pages 10–11 or have the student fill out the self-assessment on page 13 to evaluate the retelling. In addition to discussing expression and pacing, you should be sure to ask the student several questions about the meaning of the text.

Tips

Directions: First try reading this passage out loud very fast to a partner. Turn the paper over and see if your partner can figure out what a 15 percent tip would be for a bill of $15.00. Turn your paper over and try reading the passage at a slower pace. Is it easier for your partner to understand something when a person reads slowly or quickly?

> **Remember:**
> The goal of fluency isn't to read *faster*, it is to read smoothly and *with understanding*.

When you go out to eat at your favorite restaurant, chances are you leave your server a tip. Tips are important to waiters and waitresses because they make only a small amount of money per hour and rely heavily on tips to supplement this income. How much should you tip your server? The general rule is 15 percent, assuming they do a decent job. If you make a large mess or require a lot of extra attention, you should probably tip 20 percent.

So how do you determine 15 percent of your bill? There are several easy ways. Some people carry around a "tip calculator" card that gives a chart with different dollar amounts, along with the suggested tip amount for 15 and 20 percent. Other people multiply the cost of the meal by 0.15. Still others estimate what 10 percent of the bill is and then add half that amount again to come up with the tip. Leaving the right tip shows your server that you appreciate good service and hard work.

Name _____ Date _____

Fluency

comprehension, real-life reading

Directions

Directions: Have you ever read directions out loud while someone else tries to put together a new bike or some other item? Being able to read directions with fluency is an important lifelong skill. Pull out the directions for your favorite game, microwave snack, or piece of electronic equipment (such as a TV or CD player). Choose two different sets of directions. Read each one out loud. Then answer the following questions.

1. Which set of directions were you able to read the most fluently? Why?

   _____

2. Why do you think you might pause frequently when reading directions? Why do you think this is of a particular importance when reading this type of text?

   _____

3. After reading the directions, do you think you could play the game or complete the task? Why or why not? (Knowing how to pronounce all of the words doesn't always mean you can *understand* what you have read!)

   _____

4. Which directions were the most difficult to understand? Choose one set of directions and rewrite it so it is easier to read. Then try reading the directions you have written out loud. Were you able to read them with more fluency than the original directions? Why or why not?

   _____

   _____

Published by Instructional Fair. Copyright protected. 0-7424-2824-9 *Reading for Every Child: Fluency*

Dilemma

We knew Mom was really stressed from working at a new job and trying to fix up the apartment before our grandmother came to visit. One of her projects was painting her room. She was having an awful time deciding on a color.

"I think I want a peaceful feeling as if I were floating on clouds above a sunset," Mom would say. "Maybe pale lavender? No, I think maybe a dark mauve would be better—like roses in an English garden."

Then, two days later, she would say, "I just love hunter green and cream. It's so woodsy!"

Woodsy? I wondered where she was going with that.

We waited. And waited. Three days went by. Could it still be hunter green and cream?

Finally, on Thursday, the definitive answer came. "Blue. Wonderful, clean, brilliant-sky blue with white trim on the woodwork."

So that was it—Bombay Blue. She even bought the brushes, rollers, and paint.

Unfortunately, Mom had no time for painting.

My sister Katy and I came up with a plan.

"Why don't we surprise Mom and paint the room for her?" I suggested.

"I don't know Ben," pondered Katy. "You know Mom gets kind of freaky if we get into her stuff."

"Hmmmm," I replied thoughtfully. "But if she didn't know ..."

A few weeks later, snow covered the city and school was canceled. As you might imagine, we were heartbroken—NOT!

As soon as Mom left for work, we put our plan into action. We jumped into some ratty clothes, shoved her bed against another wall, covered the floor with an old sheet, and mixed and poured the paint. We were ready to begin!

Dilemma (cont.)

"Whew!" Katy groaned a short time later. "I'm wiped out!"

I sighed and rolled my eyes. "Katy, we've only been at it for fifteen minutes."

"Well, then we need to paint faster!" demanded my sister.

"To do a good job, we have to take our time," I reminded her.

After about an hour of bending, brushing, rolling, and dripping a fair amount of Bombay Blue on ourselves, we could finally see some progress.

"Not bad!" observed Katy as she stood back to admire her work.

"EEEEEK!!!" Katy backed into the pan of paint and landed in it with her right foot! There was a break in the action as I helped her hobble into the bathroom and stick her foot under the tub faucet. Then it was back to work.

We decided not to tell Mom about the wall until later that night after dinner.

"I'm home!" announced our mother as she breezed in through the front door after work. She had a pizza in one hand, her briefcase in the other, and a big smile on her face.

Katy and I exchanged knowing looks. We could hardly contain our excitement!

Mom gave us a glowing report about the townhouse she had sold that afternoon. Her boss was amazed by the deal she had put together. "I'm so happy! This new job is going to be great!" Mom was practically singing! "I feel all sunny and bright inside like a cloud has lifted from over my head! I feel ... YELLOW! That's it! My room has to be a glorious, cheery YELLOW!"

"Oh, no," muttered Katy under her breath, looking as if there were an earthquake in her stomach. She turned to me with her eyes wide open as if to say, "HELP!!!"

Fluency

Dilemma—Teacher Discussion Guide

Use the story on pages 73–74 to work with your students on fluency and comprehension skills.

1. Practice "talking the talk." Ask students how they think Katy and Ben would sound if you overheard their conversation. Practice reading aloud with the class. Pick one line of dialogue to read, and then have students read one to you as a group choral reading.

2. Choose three of the verbs from the selection that tell how someone spoke (e.g., **groaned, pondered, demanded, reminded, observed, announced, muttered**). Have students write a new sentence for that verb where someone says something to express that same emotion.

3. Have students draw three pictures of the story; one each for the beginning, middle, and end. Students write a sentence describing each picture and explain drawings to their partner. Partners compare pictures. Are they the same or different? If they are different, explain how.

4. Each partner pair should finish the story. Together, they write an ending telling what Ben, Katy, and Mom do. Partners can take turns reading the completed writing to the class.

5. Have students think of a time they faced a dilemma. Students should write about what happened, who was with them, where they were, when it happened, and how they resolved it.

6. Then students read the selection with their partner in several different ways: reading alternate lines, echo reading, choral reading.

7. Instruct each group of students to read the selection with another pair of partners as if this were a readers' theater script. The four students will need choose among the following roles—Mom, Ben, Katy, and the narrator.

Dilemma—Student Response Page

Directions: Use the story on pages 73–74 to answer the questions below. You will need to work with a partner.

1. Who is telling this story?

    a. Ben

    b. Katy

    c. Mom

2. What is the main focus of this story?

    a. problems with painting

    b. a mom who can't make up her mind

    c. a good deed that backfired

3. The story says that Katy **pondered** Ben's question. What does **pondered** mean?

    a. answered

    b. mumbled

    c. thought about

4. When Ben and Katy waited after mom decided on hunter green and cream for her room, what were they waiting for?

    a. the paint to dry

    b. Mom to be sure about her decision

    c. Mom to go and buy the paint

5. Why do you think Katy looked at Ben as if to say **"HELP!"**?

   _____

   _____

6. Make a prediction about what you think will happen next in this story.

   _____

Resources

Bibliography

Allington, R. L. *What Really Matters for Struggling Readers: Designing Research-Based Programs*. New York: Longman, 2001.

Calkins, L. M. *The Art of Teaching Reading*. New York: Longman, 2001.

Hancock, M. R. *A Celebration of Literature and Response*. Upper Saddle River, NJ: Prentice-Hall, Inc., 2000.

Hoyt, L. *Revisit, Reflect, Retell—Strategies for Improving Reading Comprehension*. Portsmouth, NH: Heinemann, 1999.

McKenna, M. C. *Help for Struggling Readers—Strategies for Grades 3–8*. New York: The Guilford Press, 2002.

Morrow, L. M., L. B. Gambrel, and M. Pressley. *Best Practices in Literacy Instruction*. New York: The Guilford Press, 2003.

National Institute for Literacy. *Put Reading First: The Research Building Blocks for Teaching Children to Read*, 2001.

Opitz, M. F., and T. V. Rasinski. *Good-bye Round Robin*. Portsmouth, NH: Heinemann, 1998.

Perfect, K. A. "Rhyme and Reason: Poetry for the heart and head." *The Reading Teacher*, 52 (1999): 728–737.

Rasinski, T. V. "Speed does matter in reading." *The Reading Teacher*, 54 (2000): 146–151.

Rasinski, T. V., and N. D. Padak. *From Phonics to Fluency*. New York: Addison, Wesley, and Longman, 2001.

Samuels, S. J. "The method of repeated readings." *The Reading Teacher*, 50 (1997): 376–381.

Poetry Collections

Bolin, F. S. ed. *Poetry for Young People—Carl Sandburg*. New York: Sterling Publishing Co. Inc., 1995.

Dakos, K. *If You're Not Here, Please Raise Your Hand: Poems About School*. New York: Four Winds Press, 1990.

Greenfield, E. *Night on Neighborhood Street*. New York: Dial, 1991.

Hopkins, L. B. *Been to Yesterdays*. Honesdale, PA: Boyds Mills Press, 1995.

Poetry Collections (cont.)

Livingston, M. C. *I Never Told and Other Poems*. New York: Macmillan, 1992.

Mavor, S. *You and Me: Poems of Friendship*. New York: Atheneum, 1997.

Nye, N. S., ed. *This Same Sky: A Collection of Poems from Around the World*. New York: Simon & Schuster, 1992.

Prelutsky, J., ed. *The 20th Century Children's Book of Poetry*. New York: Alfred A. Knopf, 1999.

Rosenberg, L., ed. *The Invisible Ladder: An Anthology of Contemporary American Poems for Young Readers*. New York: Henry Holt, 1996.

Rylant, C. *Soda Jerk*. New York: Orchard Books, 1994.

Shields, C. D. *Lunch Money and other Poems About School*. New York: Dutton, 1995.

Silverstein, S. *Where the Sidewalk Ends*. New York: Harper & Row, 1974.

Stevenson, J. *Cornflakes*. New York: Greenwillow/Harper Collins, 2000.

Viorst, J. *Sad Underwear and Other Complications*. New York: Atheneum, 1995.

Readers' Theaters

Barchers, S. L. *Scary Readers' Theater*. Englewood: Libraries Unlimited, 1994.

Bauer, C. F. *Presenting Readers' Theater*. New York: Wilson, 1987.

Dixon, N. *Learning With Readers Theater*. Winnipeg: Pegius, 1996.

Fredericks, A. D. *Frantic Frogs and Other Frankly Fractured Folktales for Readers' Theater*. Englewood: Libraries Unlimited, 1996.

Tanner, F. A. *Readers' Theater Fundamentals*. Topeka: Clark, 1993.

Titles for Two or More Readers

Fleischman, Paul. *Joyful Noise, Poems for Two Voices* (1988. New York: Harper & Row, 1988.

Hoberman, Mary Ann. *You Read to Me, I'll Read to You*. Boston: Little, Brown and Company, 2001. (It is probably geared toward younger readers but is very entertaining.)

Fluency

Best Books on Tape for Fourth-Grade Students

Fleischman, Paul. *Seek*. Read by a full cast. Listening Library.

Frady, Marshall. *Martin Luther King, Jr*. Read by Marshall Frady. Books on Tape.

Halberstam, David. *Firehouse*. Read by Mel Foster. Brilliance Audio.

Hunt, Irene. *Across Five Aprils*. Read by Terry Bregy. Audio Bookshelf.

Lewis. C. S. *The Lion, the Witch, and the Wardrobe*. Read by a full cast. Focus on the Family/Tyndale House, Family Listening.

Osborne, Mary Pope. *American Tall Tales*. Read by Scott Snively. Audio Bookshelf.

Park, Linda Sue. *A Single Shard*. Read by Graeme Malcolm. Listening Library.

Singer, Nicky. *Feather Boy*. Read by Philip Franks. Listening Library.

Spinelli, Jerry. *Maniac Magee*. Read by S. Epatha Merkerson. Listening Library.

Answer Key

Cleaning .... **page 30**

1. The speaker is probably a child because of the candy and snack wrappers, homework papers, and clothing tossed around the room.
2. The speaker is an artist who created this treasure, doesn't want to clean, and thinks closing the door would be an excellent solution.
3. a. creased
4-5. Answers will vary.

Catch Up!? .... **page 33**

1. b
2. Any reasonable explanation. Possible answer could be no; the speaker in the first stanza is too impatient to appreciate how slowly ketchup moves.
3. c
4. c

It's a Bird! It's a Plane! It's a ... Penguin? .... **page 42**

1. b
2. a
3. c
4. a

Washington and Lincoln .... **page 68**

1. c
2. a
3-5. Answers will vary

Dilemma .... **page 76**

1. a
2. c
3. c
4. b
5. She was worried Mom wouldn't like the painting they had already done.
6. Answers will vary. Ben and Katy could show Mom the wall they painted, causing Mom to change her mind.